Lost Underground

Mike Tucker ● Jonatronix

Pyramid Peril

OXFORD
UNIVERSITY PRESS

CODE Control Update:

My name is **CODE**. I am the computer that controls **Micro World**. **Team X** and **Mini** are trying to get the **CODE keys** and rescue **Macro Marvel**. My **BITEs** must stop them!

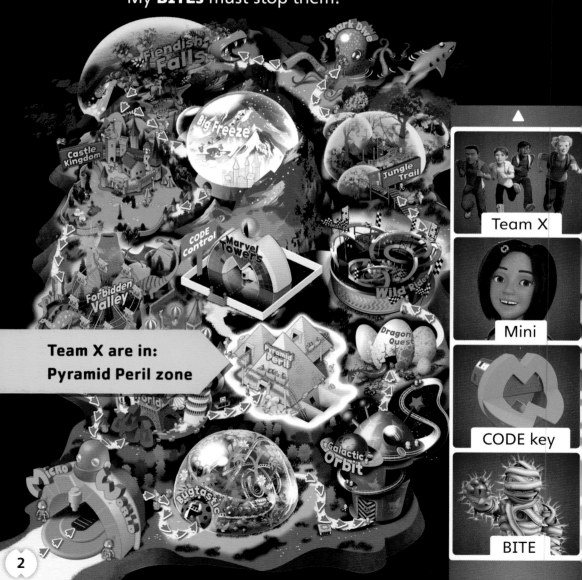

Fiendish Falls

Shark Dive

Big Freeze

Castle Kingdom

Jungle Trail

CODE Control

Marvel Towers

Wild Rides

Forbidden Valley

Team X are in:
Pyramid Peril zone

Pyramid Peril

Dragon Quest

Micro World

Bugtastic

Galactic Orbit

Team X

Mini

CODE key

BITE

2

Pyramid Peril cameras

Max, Cat, Mini and Rex were trapped in a pyramid!

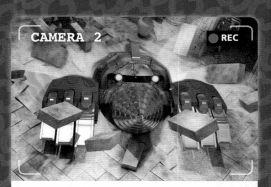

Ant and Tiger tried to rescue them in the Driller.

Then *they* were chased by the Mummy-BITE!

They escaped by shrinking and clinging on to the BITE.

Status: Max, Cat, Mini and Rex are still trapped in the pyramid.

Before you read

Sound checker

The sounds to remember when you are reading this book.

ch   y   ti   ci   ssi

Word alert

Blend the sounds. Remember the sounds you have practised.

chute   **ch**aos   hieroglyphs
direc**ti**ons   suspi**ci**on
transmi**ss**ion

Into the zone

Have you ever been in a maze? How did you find your way back out again?

Chapter 1 – Into Darkness

Max, Cat, Mini and Rex were trapped inside the pyramid.

"We need to find another way out so we can complete the mission," said Cat.

"I'll check the official guide," said Mini, looking at her Gizmo.

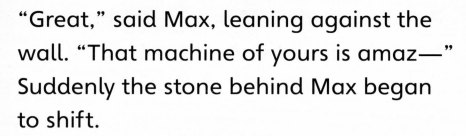

"Great," said Max, leaning against the wall. "That machine of yours is amaz—" Suddenly the stone behind Max began to shift.

"Max!" cried Cat, as her friend tumbled through a gap in the wall.

Help!

Rex darted after Max. He grabbed Max's trousers but could not stop him sliding down the steep chute.

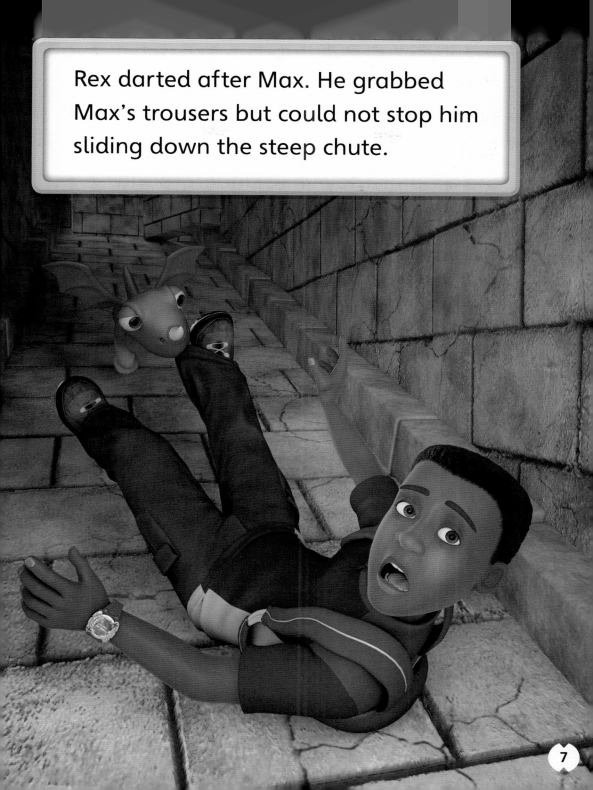

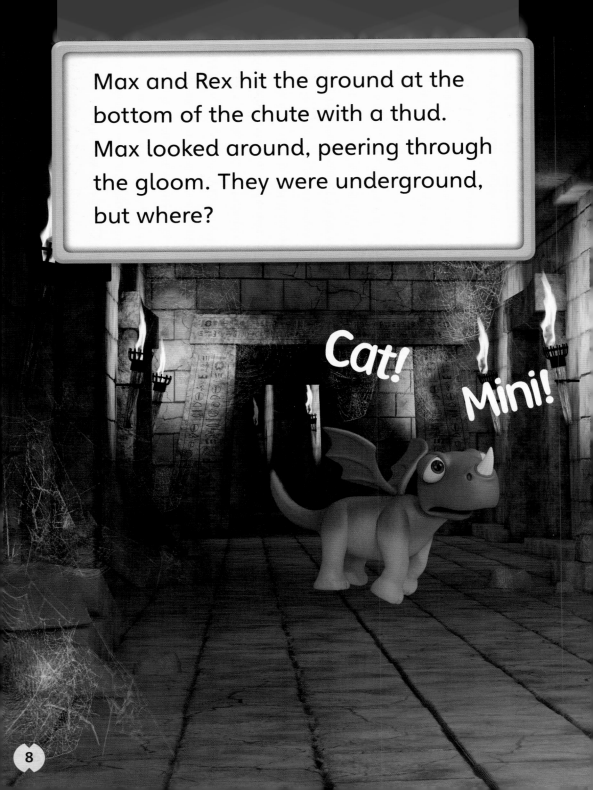

Max and Rex hit the ground at the bottom of the chute with a thud. Max looked around, peering through the gloom. They were underground, but where?

Cat!

Mini!

"Cat! Mini!" Max shouted to break the silence, but all he could hear was an echo.

"I have a horrible suspicion that we are trapped!" he said.

Chapter 2 – Lost

Just then, Max's watch flashed. It was Mini. "Max, are you both ok?" Mini's voice was faint.
"Yes," said Max, "but I can hardly hear you."

"You are in a maze," said Mini, looking at the brochure on her Gizmo. "I should be able to guide you, but I'll need a minute to work out which way you should go."

Before Mini could give Max directions, the transmission cut out. "Well, Rex, I guess it's just us," said Max bravely. "Let's try this passage."

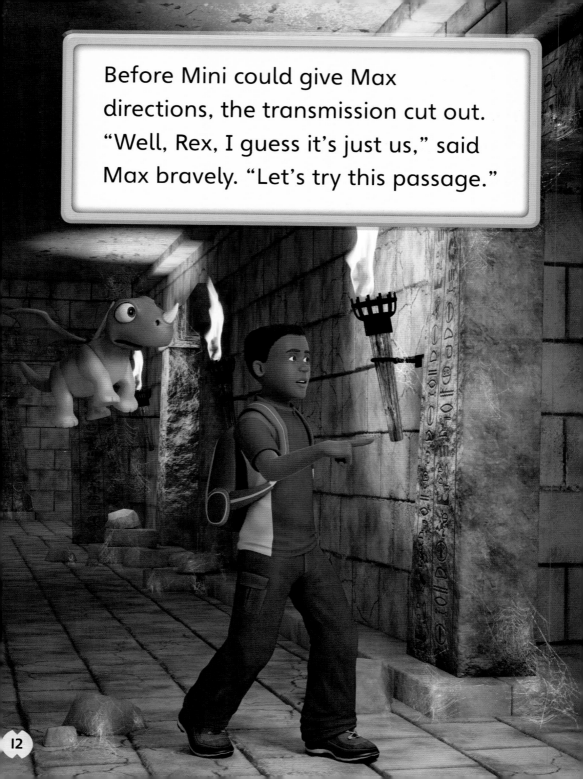

Several passages later, Max groaned in frustration as he found himself staring at another dead end.

"We need to get out before we end up as fossils!" he said.

Max sank to the ground for a rest. Suddenly, he felt a cool breeze on his hand. He looked closer to investigate. "Look, Rex! A hole!" Max cried.

They shrank and squeezed through.

Maze construction

The hole led to a huge chamber. Dozens of MITEs were moving stone blocks. "No wonder we kept getting lost," exclaimed Max. "The MITEs haven't finished the maze!"

Towards the centre of the chamber was a pillar. The pillar moved slowly down. It was carrying lots more blocks.
"It's a lift!" said Max. "The hieroglyphs must be buttons ... Let's take a closer look."

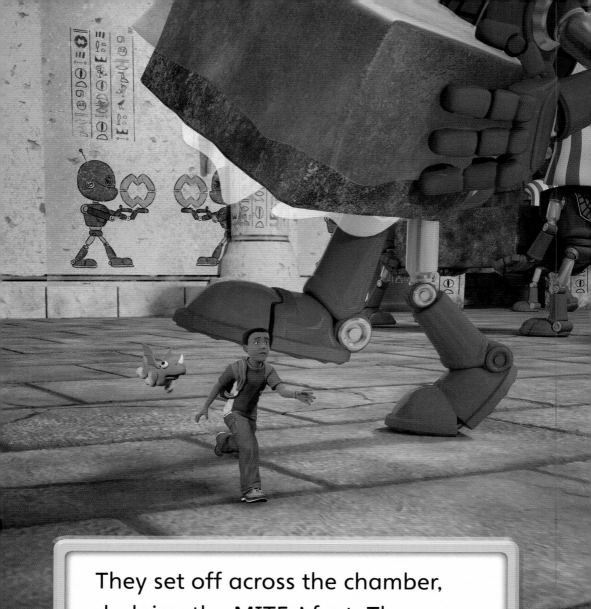

They set off across the chamber, dodging the MITEs' feet. They were nearly at the pillar when a stone block slipped from its wrapping.

THUMP!

Rex slammed into Max, pushing him to the ground. The block thumped down next to them.

"That was close," said Max. "It's chaos in here!"

At last they made it to the pillar. It was covered with hieroglyphs, including one that looked like a dinosaur! Max scratched his head as he tried to unravel the code.

Finally he spotted a symbol shaped like an arrow.

"I think that means *up*," he said to Rex. "Let's hope I'm right!"

Max grew so he was the right height to push the hieroglyph.

The pillar began to rise. Max leapt on.

Max saw Cat and Mini waiting for them at the top.

"I'm so glad to see you," laughed Max. "Especially with that cart. Mazes are seriously tiring!"

Now you have read ...
Lost Underground

Take a closer look

Max fell down the chute and ended up deep underground.
What do you think he could see, hear, touch and smell?
How do you think Max was feeling?

Thinking time

Read page 13 again. Why did Max say this?
"We need to get out before we end up as fossils!"